DOGS SET XI

AFFENPINSCHERS

Kristin Petrie
ABDO Publishing Company

visit us at
www.abdopublishing.com

Published by ABDO Publishing Company, PO Box 398166, Minneapolis, MN 55439.
Copyright © 2014 by Abdo Consulting Group, Inc. International copyrights reserved
in all countries. No part of this book may be reproduced in any form without written
permission from the publisher. The Checkerboard Library™ is a trademark and logo of
ABDO Publishing Company.

Printed in the United States of America, North Mankato, Minnesota.
102013
012014

 PRINTED ON RECYCLED PAPER

Cover Photo: Alamy
Interior Photos: Alamy pp. 9, 19, 21; Corbis pp. 7, 13, 15; iStockphoto pp. 11, 15, 17;
    SuperStock pp. 5, 17

Editors: Tamara L. Britton, Megan M. Gunderson, Bridget O'Brien
Art Direction: Neil Klinepier

Library of Congress Cataloging-in-Publication Data

Petrie, Kristin, 1970-
 Affenpinschers / Kristin Petrie.
    pages cm. -- (Dogs)
 Includes index.
 ISBN 978-1-62403-099-4
 1. Affenpinscher--Juvenile literature. I. Title.
 SF429.A34P48 2014
 636.76--dc23
                              2013025890

CONTENTS

The Dog Family 4

Affenpinschers. 6

What They're Like 8

Coat and Color. 10

Size 12

Care 14

Feeding 16

Things They Need 18

Puppies 20

Glossary 22

Web Sites. 23

Index 24

THE DOG FAMILY

What dog both looks like and is named after a monkey? The affenpinscher! In the German language, *affenpinscher* means "monkey terrier." The dog is sometimes called the affen.

In spite of its name, the affenpinscher is a member of the toy group in the **American Kennel Club (AKC)**. It is one of the AKC's 175 recognized **breeds**.

That's a lot of breeds! Why are there so many? Well, it all began when early humans trained wolf pups to help hunt game. These **domesticated** wolves were the first dogs. In fact, dogs and wolves are both members of the family **Canidae**.

As humans needed help with other work, they developed new breeds. Some dogs were big and

bold. These made good guard dogs. Others were natural hunters. Small, cuddly dogs made good companions. Today, this is the affenpinscher's job.

The affenpinscher

AFFENPINSCHERS

The affenpinscher originated in central Europe. It did not start out as a companion **breed**. It is a descendant of hunting dogs. What did the dogs hunt? Rats! They were so good at their job that they were known as Ratters.

Ratters controlled rodents around farms, stables, and stores. However, they were too big to do this work indoors. So, humans bred the Ratter with smaller breeds. This resulted in the affenpinscher. This little dog kept the house free of rodents.

In Germany, breeders continued to develop the breed. Eventually, the affenpinscher spread across Europe and to the United States. The **AKC** recognized the breed in 1936. Today, it has a small but devoted following.

Affenpinscher Banana Joe won the Best in Show award at the 2013 Westminster Kennel Club Dog Show.

WHAT THEY'RE LIKE

The name "monkey terrier" describes the affenpinscher's looks and many of its behaviors. This clever dog uses its **nimble** paws like a monkey uses its hands. For example, it can throw toys in the air and catch them!

The playful and energetic affen can also walk on its hind legs. When on all fours, the mischievous little dog may dart away with stolen items!

But despite its silly actions, the affenpinscher is territorial, independent, and bold. These qualities make the affenpinscher an excellent watchdog.

In addition, the affenpinscher has not lost its natural hunting instinct. So, keep hamsters, gerbils, and other rodent-like pets safe around this **breed**!

In France, the breed is called the Diablotin Moustachu. This means "mustached little devil"!

Coat and Color

The affenpinscher's coat is shaggy but neat. The **dense**, rough, wiry hair is one inch (2.5 cm) long on the body and shoulders. Shorter hair covers its rear end and tail. The dog's head, neck, chest, belly, and legs have longer, softer hair.

Full-grown affenpinschers have a mane around the neck. It blends into the coat on the dog's back between the shoulders. The mane, eyebrows, and beard, along with longer hair on the head, give the affenpinscher its special, monkey-like appearance.

In the past, black was the standard color for the **breed**. Today, a variety of colors are acceptable. These include black, gray, silver, red, black and tan, and **belge**. In addition, some dogs have black masks on their faces.

A black and tan affenpinscher

SIZE

The affenpinscher is just 9.5 to 11.5 inches (24 to 29 cm) tall. Both males and females weigh about 8 pounds (3.5 kg).

Despite their tiny size, the affenpinscher's body is strong and sturdy. Its compact frame is square in shape thanks to a broad chest and wide hips. The affenpinscher has a level, short back. The tail can be left natural or cropped to 1 to 2 inches (2.5 to 5 cm) in length. Its legs are straight and have medium-sized bones.

The affenpinscher's most notable feature is its face. The coat on the face and head is longer than on the rest of the body. It covers a round head topped with ears that can be cropped or natural.

The affenpinscher should not become overweight.
Extra weight will stress the little dog's joints.

A short **muzzle** narrows to a black, blunt nose. Round, deep-set eyes and a full jaw enhance the dog's monkey-like appearance.

CARE

The affenpinscher is a healthy, robust dog. However, with its short **muzzle**, this **breed** can easily become overheated. And, some affenpinschers can have joint and vision problems.

Annual visits to the veterinarian will help maintain your affen's good health. **Vaccinations** will prevent illness. The veterinarian can also **spay** or **neuter** your dog.

The affenpinscher requires home care as well. Luckily, its **dense** coat **sheds** little and is easy to groom. Weekly brushing of the longer hair is sufficient. This is a good time to trim your affen's nails. And, be sure to brush its teeth every day. This can prevent gum disease and tooth decay.

Your affen will need regular care throughout its life. The relationship your dog has with its veterinarian will be an important one.

FEEDING

The active affenpinscher needs a **nutritious** diet. Many quality dog foods are available to meet this need. These foods come in several varieties.

Dry, moist, and semimoist foods have different advantages. Moist and semimoist foods are easy to digest. They also contain water. Hard, dry foods clean a dog's teeth while it is eating. They are also less perishable and can be left out longer without spoiling.

Leaving food out all day is called free feeding. Free feeding can be a problem for the affenpinscher. This **breed** loves to eat and will devour every morsel! It is better to feed your affen small meals at regular times each day. This will help the dog maintain a healthy weight.

The young affenpinscher requires several small meals a day due to its rapid growth. Food designed for puppies is best for them. As a dog's growth slows, the amount of food it needs decreases. Adult dogs require two small or one larger meal per day. And whatever the feeding schedule, all dogs need fresh water every day.

Wet food can collect in the affen's facial hair, creating a gummy mess! Dry food can help avoid this.

THINGS THEY NEED

Dogs of all **breeds** need a few supplies. Food and water dishes, a leash, and a collar are essential. Since the affenpinscher has a short **muzzle**, shallow dishes are easier to eat from. Stainless steel and ceramic dishes are good choices. A sturdy but comfortable collar and leash will keep the affen close on long walks.

Dogs also benefit from having a crate. A crate provides a safe and cozy place for dogs to take breaks and sleep. Crates are also useful for house training and travel. Wire and plastic crates are two popular varieties.

The playful affenpinscher also needs toys. Toys can entertain an affen for hours. Toys also prevent boredom. A bored dog can cause trouble!

Training and **socialization** are also important. Expose your affen to different people, dogs, and surroundings. This will teach your dog how to behave appropriately in different situations.

Taking your affen on a long walk or hike will provide mental stimulation for this naturally curious breed!

PUPPIES

Like all dogs, the female affenpinscher is **pregnant** for about 63 days. After this time, she gives birth to one to three tiny puppies. The puppies are born blind and deaf. They depend on their mother for everything.

After 10 to 14 dark, quiet days, the puppies begin to see and hear. When they are three weeks old, the puppies begin to explore their surroundings. They naturally **wean** from their mother's milk as they eat more solid foods.

Affenpinscher puppies are ready for adoption between 12 and 16 weeks of age. If you think an affen is the right pet for your family, locate a good **breeder**. This may take some time since affens are rare.

At the **breeder**'s, look for energetic and curious puppies. They should be about the same size as their siblings. And, their eyes should be clear. These are signs of good health. Begin training and **socialization** right away. A healthy and happy affenpinscher will be a loving member of your family for 12 to 16 years!

Affenpinschers are loyal, affectionate, and protective companions.

GLOSSARY

American Kennel Club (AKC) - an organization that studies and promotes interest in purebred dogs.

belge - a color that is a mixture of black and reddish brown.

breed - a group of animals sharing the same ancestors and appearance. A breeder is a person who raises animals. Raising animals is often called breeding them.

Canidae (KAN-uh-dee) - the scientific Latin name for the dog family. Members of this family are called canids. They include wolves, jackals, foxes, coyotes, and domestic dogs.

dense - thick or compact.

domesticated - adapted to life with humans.

muzzle - an animal's nose and jaws.

neuter (NOO-tuhr) - to remove a male animal's reproductive glands.

nimble - able to move quickly, easily, and lightly.

nutritious - that which promotes growth, provides energy, repairs body tissues, and maintains life.

pregnant - having one or more babies growing within the body.

shed - to cast off hair, feathers, skin, or other coverings or parts by a natural process.

socialize - to adapt an animal to behaving properly around people or other animals in various settings.

spay - to remove a female animal's reproductive organs.

vaccine (vak-SEEN) - a shot given to prevent illness or disease.

wean - to accustom an animal to eating food other than its mother's milk.

WEB SITES

To learn more about affenpinschers, visit ABDO Publishing Company online. Web sites about affenpinschers are featured on our Book Links page. These links are routinely monitored and updated to provide the most current information available.
www.abdopublishing.com

INDEX

A
adoption 20
American Kennel Club
  4, 6

B
beard 10
body 10, 12
breeder 6, 20, 21

C
Canidae (family) 4
character 5, 8, 16,
  19, 21
coat 10, 12, 14
collar 18
color 10, 13
crate 18

E
ears 12
Europe 6
eyes 13, 14, 21

F
food 16, 17, 18, 20

G
Germany 6
grooming 14

H
head 10, 12
health 14, 21
history 4, 5, 6
hunting 6, 8

L
leash 18
legs 8, 10, 12
life span 21

M
muzzle 13, 14, 18

N
nails 14
neck 10
neuter 14
nose 13

P
paws 8
puppies 17, 20, 21

R
reproduction 20

S
senses 14, 20
shedding 14
size 6, 12, 21
socialization 19, 21
spay 14

T
tail 10, 12
teeth 14, 16
toys 8, 19
training 18, 19, 21

U
United States 6

V
vaccines 14
veterinarian 14

W
water 16, 17, 18